Old Wombwell (and Heming

by

Chris and Pearl Sharp

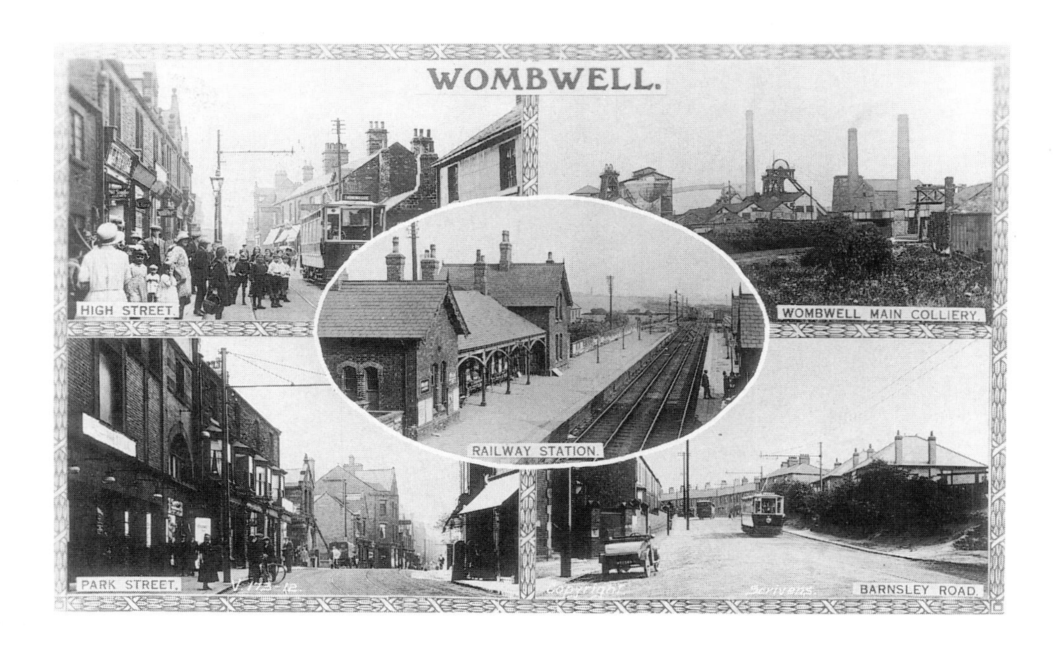

A multi-view postcard of Wombwell with (top left) a Thurnscoe bound tram drawing an interested crowd of spectators. Four councils united in the construction and operation of the light railway to carry passengers from Thurnscoe to Barnsley via Goldthorpe, Bolton-on-Dearne, Wath and Wombwell. It was the last tramway system to be built and operated from 1924 until 1933, but it was not until 1960 that the trams and tramway were finally paid for.

First Published in the United Kingdom, 1994
By Richard Stenlake, Ochiltree Sawmill, The Lade, Ochiltree, Ayrshire KA18 2NX
Telephone: 01290 700266

ISBN 1-872074-46-4

This photograph was taken at the junction of Myrtle Street and Barnsley Road. On the land to the left was Diggles' Garage, now replaced by Harratts Volvo Garage

FOREWORD

by

Don Walton

Being very much dependent on the coal-mining industry, Wombwell, like other towns in the North of England, has seen many changes. Wombwell Main, Darfield Main, Mitchell Main and Cortonwood Collieries provided jobs for most of the work force. Subsidiary industries such as the Brickworks, Wombwell Foundry and the Chemical Works also helped to keep the area a thriving centre during the period these photographs depict.

Shops have changed hands and upper floors have become storerooms or offices in place of living quarters for the town's shopkeepers. The roads have become much busier with motor traffic. Gone are the horses and carts and the trams. Roads have been widened and buildings demolished.

The street scenes of Hemingfield also reflect changes. Whole rows of houses have gone and even a place of worship has disappeared.

Within a short time now, personal recollections of the scenes from the beginning of the century shown in this book will have gone forever, but the photographers of that time have left us a permanent record of what has been.

A crowd of children gathered at the bottom of Cemetery Road. The uniformed policeman with his white gloves appears to be in charge.

The building in the distance was Charlesworth's farm which had a large garden to the front of the house in which grew rhubarb. Elderly citizens of Wombwell recall childhood memories of receiving a clip round the ear from the farmer for attempting to help themselves. The premises were later turned into a milk bar selling delicious home-made ice cream. It was also a fish and chip shop at one time.

Left: The Primitive Methodist Connection Church, dedicated to the memory of Henry Adams, a notable methodist, has five memorial stones laid by Mrs Henry Adams and dedicated to various members of the family. the church is now the Dentonia School of Dancing.

Right: Wombwell Town Hall was originally built without the corner balcony, which was added later. The foundation stone was laid by Mrs Mitchell of Bolton Hall in June 1902. A Boer War Memorial is situated on the Station Lane side of the building. The original gas lamps are still attached to the frontage. Gas lighting was installed in Wombwell in 1870 and the town's last gas lamp was situated at the High Street end of Alma Street.

HIGH STREET, WOMBWELL.

In this 1918 view of the High Street, the store to the top of Station Lane is G H Spedding, Drapery and Hosiery, offering Dress Skirts for sale from 3/11 to 30/- (very expensive!). The building to the left, Guest's Outfitters, is now the Churchill Hotel.

The High Street in 1912 showing Guest's Outfitters with a snicket up the side of the shop giving access to the pawnbrokers. The snicket also led to Barn Row, a terrace of stone flag roofed buildings.

The War Memorial built of Portland Stone is shown on the left of this 1928 postcard view. It was constructed to commemorate the victims of the First World War. Their names were finely etched in the stone, but have now worn away. The memorial was unveiled in 1920 by Captain Wentworth of Stainborough Castle and was enlarged to record the dead of the Second World War.

HIGH STREET. WOMBWELL. (NO. 2)

According to the message on the back of this 1928 postcard the fellow marked with the cross was on his way to collect his dole when he was snapped by the camera!

Taylors Chemists had a large weighing machine inside the doorway. The premises are now occupied by Z A Akram.

The buildings on the left are still standing. Adron's shop is now divided into a fashion shop, a building society and the DSS. The next building along, with the ornate stone frontage, is now the Carpet Shop, but previously was the Co-op butchery, drapery and boot department. The decorative building on the right with the corner facing window was the Co-op grocery department. The Wombwell Co-operative Society existed before the Barnsley Co-operative, but was bought out by the latter in 1866.

High Street showing the Co-op drapery department on the left. This is now the Show Boat Building although the iron facade no longer exists. A plaque on the side of the building denotes that it once was the Co-op.

The low building on the right was Wainwrights newsagents. Access was gained down steps into the shop. The next building along was the ' Meat Emporium'.

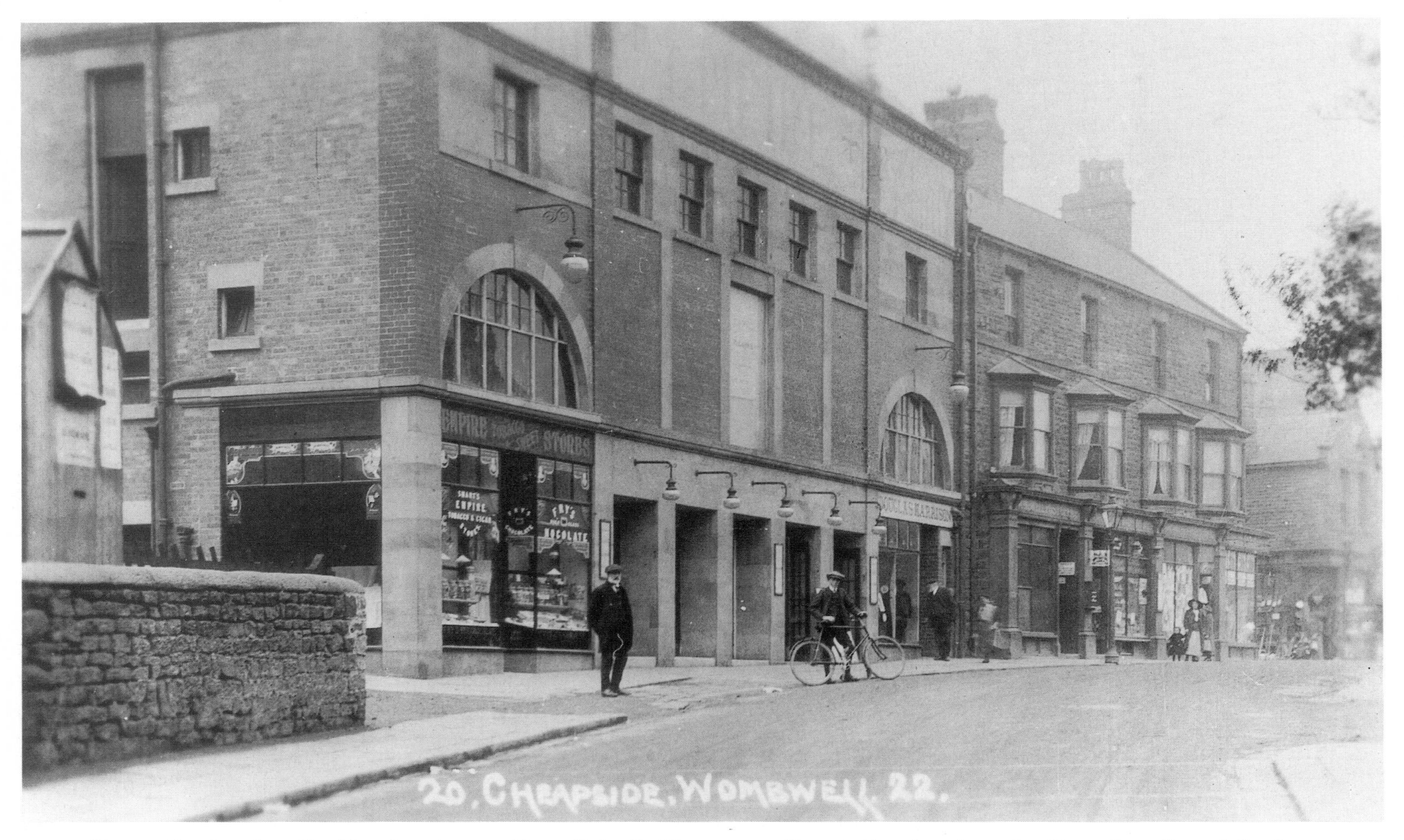

Cheapside showing the Empire cinema (demolished). The new police station has been built on the site set further back from the road.

This 1925 view of Park Street shows the Salvation Army Citadel on the left which replaced a building in Station Lane which had been demolished because of mining subsidence. The Conservative Club, completed in 1888, is on the right. The next building on that side was once the Methodist Chapel and now Wombwell Thespians Playhouse.

Behind the trees on the right is the impressive brick-built Wombwell Grange, now the premises of M P Burke the civil engineering company. The building beyond is a private residence, Brantwood, built in 1904. Over the wall on the left is Wombwell Hall

Park Street runs into Wath Road. On the land to the left now stands the Countryman Public House.

This photgraph was taken in 1908, before the Salvation Army Citadel was built.

The 'Bottom' station which was next to the gas works. All that remains of the station is the ticket office, now the Railway Inn. During Doncaster race weeks children would wait in the station yard for the trains returning from Doncaster. Men who had been to the races and won would bring Doncaster butterscotch to give to the eagerly awaiting children. Times were hard for poor families and people were willing to share when they had any good fortune.

This view of Station Lane taken in the 1930s shows Beardshall's barbers shop and Diggles' Outfitters and Furnishers. Lower down is the Salvation Army building constructed in 1910. In the distance is the bridge over the canal.

COPYRIGHT WML 2 STATION ROAD, WOMBWELL LILYWHITE LTD. ALL BRITISH PHOTO PRINTERS

Beyond the public library we can see Taylors Printers premises with a billboard advertising Baileys Furnishers of New Street, Barnsley. Before the railway arrived in Wombwell this lane was called Well Lane. Beardshall's barbers shop is on the right. Is that Mr Beardshall himself standing in the doorway?

The bridge over the canal. The Dearne and Dove Canal took eleven years to build and was opened in 1804. In 1964 it was filled in and the roundabout on the by-pass now stands on the site. The building to the left of the bridge is the working mens' club, reputed to sell the cheapest beer in England!

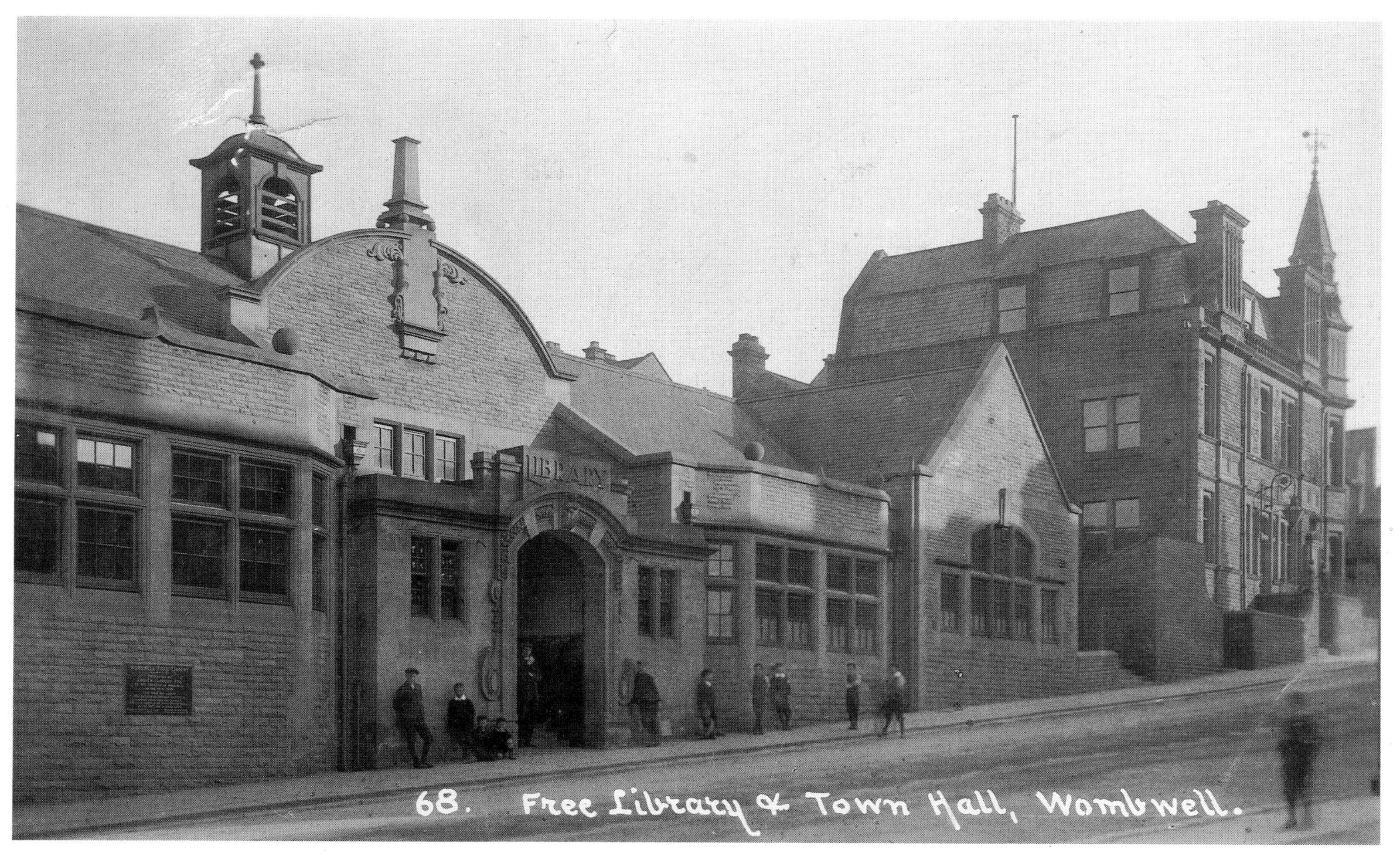

This postcard, posted in 1908, shows the public library constructed in 1905 with money donated by the Carnegie Foundation. The library, which has suffered widespread subsidence damage, is built on the site of the well which gave Wombwell its name.

The Royal Oak, Hough Lane was demolished in stages and the new Royal Oak built around it to prevent loss of the licence. The building up from the church was the Church of England School and is now a community hall, although the frontage has been altered. The church tower was erected in 1914 (after these photographs had been taken) and was capped off in 1960. The previous church which stood on the same site dated back to 1170.

The Reform Club is on the left in this photograph of the lower end of Hough Lane. The Register Office is also shown.

Hough Lane is the main road to Sheffield. The terraced and detached properties date from the late nineteenth century.

The Baths building in Hough Lane. Higher up can be seen the Hippodrome Picture Palace, known also as the 'penny rush'. Previously the Hippodrome had been a music hall and artists were housed at various lodgings in Hough Lane. At one time the building was also a skating rink. Gas masks were issued to the people of Wombwell from here at the beginning of the Second World War. It was subsequently demolished and an air-raid shelter was built on the site.

Although railings exist today in front of the houses on the right, they are not the original ones, those having been taken for scrap metal in the war effort. A plaque over numbers 68 and 70 tells us that 'Melton View' was built in 1901.

The Sir George's Arms in Hough Lane with Mr T Connelly Fruit and Vegetable Merchant's horse and cart parked outside. Mr Connelly worked at Cortonwood Colliery and saved up ten guineas to buy his first horse and cart (the one shown in the photograph), the bridles and reins and his first load of stock from Dennis of Barnsley. He later went on to acquire more horses and carts and shop premises. The family was in business for seventy years, his daughter, Ivy Camm, taking over the business, which was based in Ship's Yard, in 1950.

The bandstand in Wombwell Park. The park consisted of forty acres, with one part known as the dingle reached by steps, and also a garden of remembrance.

The railway first reached Wombwell in 1840 with the first route from Mexboro and Wath travelling through Wombwell to Barnsley and Penistone. A branch line of the Midland Railway was opened in 1899, the route being from Sheffield to Barnsley and on to Wakefield. This station is still in use today, on the Sheffield to Leeds route.

The coal industry came to Wombwell about the mid nineteenth century. The oldest pits were Wombwell Main and Darfield Main. Mitchell Main was sunk in 1870 (the owner was Joseph Mitchell).

Coal was Wombwell's first industry and when the canal was cut the coal trade expanded as boats brought props for the pits and sand for the glass works, returning with coal for the ports or for use in the Sheffield steel industry.

Mitchell Main rescue team and their equipment. Each colliery had one or more rescue teams in proportion to the number of men who were employed at the mine. One of Wombwell's worst mine disasters happened at Lundhill Colliery in 1857. One hundred and eighty nine men and boys were killed.

Wombwell Main was owned by Charles Bartholomew, to whom a memorial exists in the church. The mine's worst recorded disaster was an underground fire in 1862, although no lives were lost. The pit, the largest employer in the area, closed in 1969.

Cortonwood Colliery was sunk in 1873 and was the first of the Wombwell collieries to close following the year long miners' strike of 1984.

Wombwell Chemical Works where cosmetics and patent medicines were manufactured.

The Littlefield Lane Crossing rail pile-up was one of the worst disasters that ever happened in Wombwell. It occurred on December 13th 1911.

Waggons loaded with coal broke away down Sheffield Bank, the section of the line which ran from Dovecliffe to Mitchell Main. Near Dovecliffe the guard jumped clear fracturing his leg. The train careered down the line towards Wombwell. The signalman had to quickly decide whether to throw the switch and derail the train or allow it to carry on to Wombwell, where a train carrying Grammar School pupils was due. He pulled the switch and the train piled up.

The driver, Lion Wallis, was pinned under the engine and died soon after being rescued. The fireman, Bernard Allen, was also killed.

Wombwell Wood belonged to Earl Fitzwilliam and was well stocked with game. It was closely guarded by gamekeepers. Badgers and squirrels were in abundance. Every year local miners assisted as bush beaters at the pheasant shoot. In 1906 the day's bag totalled 1096 pheasants, 20 hares, 16 foxes and wood pigeons and rabbits by the hundreds.

This tree was known locally as 'the rocking tree'. It must have been a Sunday, this day in 1906 when the party of 'walkers' were photographed. All four have their pocket watch alberts across their waiscoats and flat caps and best suits were hardly the wear for tree climbing!

A charming scene as the ladies pause for a rest by the stile during another Sunday walk near Wombwell Woods. Five ladies and all wearing their best hats!

The Wesleyan Church had a large following in the Wombwell area. In this photograph the crowds gather to witness the laying of the foundation stone of the new Wesleyan Sunday School at Wombwell in 1904.

A crowd is once more gathered, this time to witness the laying of the foundation stone for the new chancel at Wombwell Church. The church was built between 1896 and 1898 and the chancel was completed in 1905.

A Wombwell Church outing to Cawthorne Park early this century. Such outings were happy occasions . Many chara-banc parties took picnics or called at tearooms

Hemingfield, the twenty-eighth branch of the Barnsley British Co-operative Society, opened in 1884. Many of our older readers will remember the skilful way that numerous odd-shaped groceries were packed, wrapped and tied with brown paper and string into neat parcels by the shop assistants.

A view, taken higher up Cemetery Road than the Milton Arms, showing the now demolished Top Row, a row of houses that was set at right angles to the main road.

The Milton Arms, a Bentley's house, now The Fiddlers, in Cemetery Road. The wall between the two blocks has disappeared and the street lighting has changed.

Looking down Cemetery Road from the railway bridge. The horse and cart was the usual means of carrying, delivering or selling on the streets.

A fine group of members of the Wesleyan Chapel and Sunday School gathered with festive decorations outside their place of worship in School Street. Sadly, the Chapel is now demolished.

For a small village, Hemingfield Wesleyan Sunday School had a good following and with the manual organ would be in great voice. The superb banner would be carried in procession at Whitsuntide.